AN ACROSTIC FOR YOU

Poetic Stars

Edited By Allie Jones

First published in Great Britain in 2021 by:

Young Writers
Remus House
Coltsfoot Drive
Peterborough
PE2 9BF
Telephone: 01733 890066
Website: www.youngwriters.co.uk

Printed and bound in the UK by BookPrintingUK
Website: www.bookprintinguk.com
YB0455L

Foreword

Dear Reader,

Welcome to a fun-filled book of acrostic poems!

Here at Young Writers, we are delighted to introduce our new poetry competition for pupils aged 5-7 years, An Acrostic For You. Acrostic poems are an enjoyable way to introduce pupils to the world of poetry and allow the young writers to open their imaginations to a range of topics of their choice. The engaging worksheets allowed even the youngest (or most reluctant) of writers to create a poem using the acrostic technique, and with that, encouraged them to include other literary techniques such as similes and description. Here at Young Writers we are passionate about introducing the love and art of creative writing to the next generation and we love being a part of their journey.

From family to teachers, from pets to popstars, these pupils have shaped and crafted their ideas brilliantly, showcasing their budding creativity as they celebrate the people that are important to them. More than ever it's important to show our appreciation to the people who do so much for us, and these young poets are a shining example of how to do just that. We hope you will delight in these poems as much as we have.

Contents

Broughton Infant School, Aylesbury

Eshaal Hammad (7) — 1
Jack Kiddle (6) — 2
Ella Cornwell (6) — 3
Percy Richardson (6) — 4
Leah Philbey (6) — 5
Anaya Naeem (6) — 6
Cristian Sabau (6) — 7
Talia Smith (7) — 8
Zakariah Jackson-Smith (6) — 9
Isabel Lucas (6) — 10
Vaishnavi Arunkumar — 11
Aleeza Raza (7) — 12
Tabitha Steward (6) — 13
Sonika Dhawan (6) — 14
Isla Russell-Bowyer (6) — 15
Lina Souidi (6) — 16
Jaxon Tullett-Wilson (6) — 17
Louie Serradimigni (6) — 18
Bob Dixon-Lowe (6) — 19
Brogyn Whittle-Murphy — 20
Adrian Mutasa (6) — 21
Mason Baron (6) — 22
Rhys Butcher — 23
Maira Saqib (6) — 24
Ayaan Ali (6) — 25
Reuben Wilson (6) — 26
Ivie Short (6) — 27
Elliot Jones (6) — 28
Jack Millward (7) — 29
Grace Powell (6) — 30
Esmae Spokes (6) — 31
Humnah Naveed (6) — 32
Manni Taylor (6) — 33

Tianna Adefila (7) — 34
Noah Fox (6) — 35
Stanley Staszewski (6) — 36
Denis Sabau (6) — 37
Jason Adeleke (7) — 38
Daniel Dedjula (7) — 39
Perry Lawford (6) — 40
Amana Raja (6) — 41
Bonni Kingham (7) — 42
Skye Sivapalan (6) — 43
Alfie Butler (6) — 44
Kyle Hobbs (6) — 45
Temi Liadi (6) — 46
Thomas Kinnard (6) — 47
Skyla Thompson (6) — 48
Drew Lindars (6) — 49

Hampton Pre-Prep And Prep School, Hampton

Ronak Banerjee (6) — 50
Felix Payne (6) — 51
Keyan Tomgusehan (6) — 52
Henry Nguyen (6) — 53
Thomas Double (6) — 54
Fin Meehan (6) — 55
Aubin Williams (7) — 56
Noah Regis (6) — 57
Max Xia (6) — 58
Sam Wiggins (6) — 59
Mahir Olcer (6) — 60
Alfie Seward (7) — 61
Jack Morris (7) — 62
Theo Constanti (6) — 63
Tommy Nicholson (6) — 64

Robin Hood Primary School, Bestwood Park

Lexie-Mae Shread (7)	65
Shiloh Howard-Reid (6)	66
Vyara Yotova (7)	67
Amy Jarzabek (6)	68
Lauren Clements (6)	69
Sehrish Dad	70
Nathaniel Oyasope (7)	71
Alexander Mitroi (7)	72
Elijah Divall (6)	73
Ashanti Bartley (6)	74
Summer-Leigh Gwynne (6)	75
Amir Manssour (6)	76
Destiny Stephens (7)	77
Lacie Harvey (6)	78
Rico Lowe (6)	79
Yishai Olaru (6)	80
Eli Park-Spencer (6)	81
Hunter Simpson (6)	82
Thomas Waterfall (6)	83
Thomas Bush (6)	84
Lena Brzozowska (6)	85
Chloe Hickling (6)	86
Alex Momoh (6)	87
Megan Gadsby (6)	88
James Kpessinlo (6)	89
La'Mour Campbell-Tucker	90
Milly Majstrowicz (6)	91
Ellie Walters (6)	92
Mason Shelborne (6)	93
Esohe Irughe (7)	94
Leah-Mai Haywood (6)	95
Harley Finch (6)	96
Eva-Lee Hallam (6)	97
Sienna Tomlinson (7)	98
Tarlia Bown (6)	99
Thomas Morley (6)	100
Jenson Bentley (6) & Spencer McLean (6)	101
Demilee Betts (6), Cooper Carter-White (6) & Thomas Singleton (7)	102
Tyler Singer (6)	103
Joakim Sei (7)	104
Lilly Papworth (6), Andrea, Nevaeh & Maia Goslawski (6)	105

St Andrew's CE Primary School, Shifnal

Edward Murphy (6)	106
Rowan Oates (5)	107
Luka Brazier (5)	108
Bethany Deavall (6)	109
Jasper Edwards (6)	110
Emiko Leese (6)	111
Phoebe Clarke (7)	112
Ben Whale (5)	113
Hattie Brettle (6)	114
Charlie Callis (5)	115
Will Elsmore-Roberts (5)	116
Hettie Middleton (6)	117
Oliver Snowdon-Cox (6)	118
Evie Stanford (6)	119
Mia Gailey (6)	120
James Simpson (7)	121
Alfie Danby (6)	122
Louise Pearson (6)	123
Bea Edwards Sherwood (6)	124
Alfie Ashley (6)	125
Eden Hateley (6)	126
Molly-May Chapman (7)	127
Isabella Turner (5)	128
Ivy Hawkes (6)	129
Liam Simpson (5)	130
Jack Parry (6)	131
Oliver Poole (6)	132
Joanna Doyle (5)	133
Leo Stevens (6)	134
Alfie Tappenden (5)	135
William Drew (5)	136
Alfie Stanford (6)	137
Louie Harris (7)	138
Penny Robinson (5)	139
William Fellows (5)	140
Sia Archontis-Soultana (5)	141

Freya Gallimore (5)	142		Amber Handley (7)	182
Alfie Evans (6)	143		Thomas-Jay Kennedy (6)	183
Charlie Jones (5)	144		Ekam Dhaliwal (6)	184
Kasper Giddings (5)	145		Riley Hayes (7)	185
Riley Setter (6)	146		Ava Worgan (6)	186
Faith Hepburn (5)	147		Jessica Hammond (6)	187
Yonni Saffhill (5)	148		Theo Harris (6)	188
Eve Kolaric (6)	149		Paige Cooper (6)	189
Luke Hayward (6)	150			
Daisy Davis (5)	151			
Edward Jackson (6)	152			
Olivia Hartshorn-Jones (5)	153			
Connie Morgans Sharples (6)	154			
Drew Hodgkisson (5)	155			
Cooper Arnold (5)	156			
Finley Hanwell	157			
Jacob Morris (6)	158			
Lola Underwood (6)	159			
Lauren Owen (6)	160			
Olivia Timon (5)	161			

Woodlands Academy Of Learning, Willenhall

Erin Stead (6)	162
Tyler Godwin (7)	163
Noah Davies-Johnson (6)	164
Chante Richards (6)	165
Jorgie Moore-Butler (6)	166
Zack Dempsey (6)	167
Isabelle Smith (6)	168
Poppy Bird (7)	169
Ivy Young (6)	170
Tallulah Webster (7)	171
Rosie Morris (7)	172
Poppy Jackson (6)	173
Amelia Parke (6)	174
Mia Phillips (6)	175
Harry Edwards (6)	176
Isaac Julie (6)	177
Emily Davies (7)	178
Lydia Bate (6)	179
Oliver Clare (7)	180
Eloise Wainwright (6)	181

The
Poems

Big Ben

B ell rings so loud
I t can be annoying
G iant tower, you might find it will fall

B ig Ben, it's so nice to be there
E lizabeth likes going there
N ovember you should be there because it's nearly Christmas!

Eshaal Hammad (7)
Broughton Infant School, Aylesbury

London Eye

L ovely and shiny
O nly spins around
N ext to the Thames
D oesn't stop
O h it's fun
N o, it's too high

E very time fun
Y ou might get scared
E veryone goes on.

Jack Kiddle (6)
Broughton Infant School, Aylesbury

The Bridge

B right in the big night

R ight in the bright night

I n the incredible night

D azzling night, calming night

G herkin is the best

E veryone loves London Bridge!

Ella Cornwell (6)

Broughton Infant School, Aylesbury

London

L ondon Bridge

O vercrowded London really is

N ever-ending London Eye

D azzling

O n the Underground it must be loud and exciting

N o one escapes the Dungeons!

Percy Richardson (6)

Broughton Infant School, Aylesbury

London Eye

L ights
O n the world
N ever stops
D eep
O ver the water
N ear Big Ben

E veryone sees it
Y ou go round
E normous.

Leah Philbey (6)
Broughton Infant School, Aylesbury

Big Ben

B ig Ben is beautiful
I n Big Ben there are bells
G iant tower like Big Ben

B ig Ben has beautiful gold
E normous towers at London
N oisy bells.

Anaya Naeem (6)
Broughton Infant School, Aylesbury

Big Ben

B ig Ben is lovely
I nside there are stairs
G old is shiny and bright

B ig Ben is busy
E veryone loves the Queen
N o one yells.

Cristian Sabau (6)
Broughton Infant School, Aylesbury

Big Ben

B ell is big

I ncredible Big Ben

G reat building

B rilliant Big Ben

E lizabeth Tower is part of Big Ben

N ight is bright.

Talia Smith (7)

Broughton Infant School, Aylesbury

Big Ben

B ig Ben
I n Big Ben it is beautiful
G herkin

B ig Ben is cool
E ntering Big Ben is cool
N ight-time makes things bright.

Zakariah Jackson-Smith (6)
Broughton Infant School, Aylesbury

London Bridge

B right lights
R eading in London library
I nteresting sights
D ogs walking in the park
G reat buildings
E xcellent trains.

Isabel Lucas (6)
Broughton Infant School, Aylesbury

Thames

T all and wide
H uge bridges and deep water
A wesome boats
M assive London Bridge
E normous bridges
S harp London Bridge.

Vaishnavi Arunkumar
Broughton Infant School, Aylesbury

Big Ben

B ig, beautiful and tall
I n the clock is round
G reat, massive

B ig, sharp points
E normous
N ight it lights up.

Aleeza Raza (7)
Broughton Infant School, Aylesbury

Big Ben

B ig precious clock
I mportant clock
G iant clock

B ig Ben makes a bong!
E normous clock
N aughty, noisy clock.

Tabitha Steward (6)

Broughton Infant School, Aylesbury

Gherkin

G reat

H ow does it work?

E veryone loves the Gherkin

R eally tall

K ind of scary

I s

N ice at night-time.

Sonika Dhawan (6)
Broughton Infant School, Aylesbury

Big Ben

B ig beautiful Ben
I s enormous
G lass windows

B usy London
E verywhere is amazing
N ice people.

Isla Russell-Bowyer (6)
Broughton Infant School, Aylesbury

London

L ondon is so bright in the night
O n the bridge
N oisy people
D azzling sky
O ver the buildings
N ever quiet.

Lina Souidi (6)
Broughton Infant School, Aylesbury

Big Ben

B usy in London
I t is important
G iant tower

B oats are busy on water
E xciting Big Ben
N oisy bells.

Jaxon Tullett-Wilson (6)
Broughton Infant School, Aylesbury

London

L ondon has metal

O utside are lots of towers

N ight is shiny

D own to the ground

O n the train

N oisy.

Louie Serradimigni (6)
Broughton Infant School, Aylesbury

Big Ben

B ig Ben is tall
I t's big
G ood clock

B ig Ben is humungous
E very day it ticks
N oisy clock!

Bob Dixon-Lowe (6)
Broughton Infant School, Aylesbury

London

L ively London

O h wow!

N ever-ending London Eye

D ark and drizzling

O h round and round

N ever stopping.

Brogyn Whittle-Murphy
Broughton Infant School, Aylesbury

The Shard

S hiny in the hidden night
H idden a little bit
A mazing things to see
R egular old building
D ark in the night.

Adrian Mutasa (6)

Broughton Infant School, Aylesbury

Big Ben

B ig
I nside Big Ben you can go high
G iant and massive

B iggest tower in London
E pic
N oisy.

Mason Baron (6)

Broughton Infant School, Aylesbury

London Bridge

B ridge is so pretty

R eally big

I nteresting place

D ogs walk on it

G reat views

E xcellent sight.

Rhys Butcher
Broughton Infant School, Aylesbury

London

L ondon is big

O n the buses

N ight lights

D own on the trains

O n the water boats

N ow it's quiet.

Maira Saqib (6)

Broughton Infant School, Aylesbury

Big Ben

B right light

I n the night

G reat

B uildings

E verywhere

N obody hates London.

Ayaan Ali (6)

Broughton Infant School, Aylesbury

Big Ben

B eautiful towers
I love it
G reat buildings

B arking dogs
E xcellent lights
N ever ends.

Reuben Wilson (6)
Broughton Infant School, Aylesbury

Big Ben

B eautiful

I mportant

G iant building

B ig shiny clock

E normous clock

N ice gold colour.

Ivie Short (6)

Broughton Infant School, Aylesbury

The Shard

S uper duper
H igh as the sky
A very at the top
R avens flying in the sky
D iamonds sparkle like the Shard.

Elliot Jones (6)

Broughton Infant School, Aylesbury

Big Ben

B ell ringing
I nteresting
G ood Big Ben

B ig Ben
E lizabeth Tower
N ight is so bright.

Jack Millward (7)
Broughton Infant School, Aylesbury

London

L ively London
O h it's so pretty at
N ight, it's so
D ark at night
O vercrowded
N ever quiet.

Grace Powell (6)

Broughton Infant School, Aylesbury

London

L ovely London

O h so bright in the

N ight

D ark and wonderful

O h so bright at

N ight!

Esmae Spokes (6)

Broughton Infant School, Aylesbury

Big Ben

B ell ringing
I nteresting
G ood

B ig Ben
E lizabeth Tower
N ight is so bright.

Humnah Naveed (6)

Broughton Infant School, Aylesbury

Big Ben

B eautiful
I nside it's huge
G old around the clock

B right
E normous
N ice.

Manni Taylor (6)
Broughton Infant School, Aylesbury

The Shard

S harp top
H as see-through glass
A tall building
R eally beautiful
D own below deep water.

Tianna Adefila (7)

Broughton Infant School, Aylesbury

Big Ben

B ig Ben
I ncredible
G reat

B ell
E lizabeth Tower
N ovember remember.

Noah Fox (6)

Broughton Infant School, Aylesbury

The Shard

S hiny building
H ard Shard
A mazing Shard
R eally tall Shard
D o cool stuff in London.

Stanley Staszewski (6)
Broughton Infant School, Aylesbury

Big Ben

B ell
I ncredible
G herkin

B ig
E lizabeth Tower
N ew buildings.

Denis Sabau (6)
Broughton Infant School, Aylesbury

Big Ben

B id sharp top
I mportant
G iant

B usy
E normous top
N ice gold.

Jason Adeleke (7)
Broughton Infant School, Aylesbury

Shard

S hiny Shard

H uge Shard

A mazing Shard

R eally tall Shard

D ark shiny blue Shard.

Daniel Dedjula (7)

Broughton Infant School, Aylesbury

Big Ben

B ig
I n the tower
G reat

B uildings
E verywhere
N ight shines.

Perry Lawford (6)
Broughton Infant School, Aylesbury

Big Ben

B eautiful colour
I mportant
G lass

B usy
E normous
N oisy.

Amana Raja (6)
Broughton Infant School, Aylesbury

The Thames

T all bridge
H uge and long
A mazing
M assive
E normous
S o loud!

Bonni Kingham (7)

Broughton Infant School, Aylesbury

Eye

E lizabeth Tower is part of Big Ben

Y ou might enjoy London

E lizabeth Tower is part of Big Ben.

Skye Sivapalan (6)

Broughton Infant School, Aylesbury

The Thames

T all, deep and wide

H uge

A ncient

M assive

E normous

S oaking.

Alfie Butler (6)

Broughton Infant School, Aylesbury

Big Ben

B ig
I t is huge
G reat

B ell
E normous
N ightmare.

Kyle Hobbs (6)
Broughton Infant School, Aylesbury

The Shard

S hiny lights
H uge building
A mazing
R eally busy
D eep inside.

Temi Liadi (6)

Broughton Infant School, Aylesbury

London

L ight

O h so dark

N ight

D ark

O h so dark

N ight.

Thomas Kinnard (6)

Broughton Infant School, Aylesbury

The Shard

S hard is big
H uge
A large tower
R eflective
D eep.

Skyla Thompson (6)

Broughton Infant School, Aylesbury

The Shard

S unny

H ot

A tower

R eflects the sun

D iamonds.

Drew Lindars (6)

Broughton Infant School, Aylesbury

Neil Armstrong

N o way of stopping him
E very step, he can do it
I t was epic for him, he is so
L ovely

A stronaut, he is a
R esilient man, he is
M arvellous nothing can
S top him. He is
T enacious, he is a
R obust man. He had lots of
O pportunites. He was
N avigating the lunar model. He is
G reat!

Ronak Banerjee (6)
Hampton Pre-Prep And Prep School, Hampton

Ginger

G oing under toys and hay with the greatest of ease

I n and out of newspaper

N ever getting in trouble whatever she does

G oing to her little drinking bottle every day

E ating lots of vegetables from her food bowl

R acing around everywhere.

Felix Payne (6)

Hampton Pre-Prep And Prep School, Hampton

Death Eater

V ile

O mnivore

L ock

D eath Eater monster

E ats a bit

M ade of pure evil

O pen

R aider of everything

T omb will not fit him when he dies.

Keyan Tomgusehan (6)

Hampton Pre-Prep And Prep School, Hampton

Messi

M essi is a good football player
E very day he plays football
S uper goals are scored by Messi
S pecial trophies are given to him
I t is a very special game to him, football.

Henry Nguyen (6)

Hampton Pre-Prep And Prep School, Hampton

My Dog

P oppy is soft

O n Poppy's birthday she got a toy monkey

P oppy is not allowed chocolate it is bad for her

P oppy is good and sometimes naughty

Y es, Poppy loves walks.

Thomas Double (6)

Hampton Pre-Prep And Prep School, Hampton

My Dog

G eordie is my dog
E ats raw meat
O ften sleeps on his head
R acing around the garden madly!
D elightful he is
I nteresting he is!
E nergy he has

Fin Meehan (6)
Hampton Pre-Prep And Prep School, Hampton

Bryher

B ryher is soft and cuddly
R ough with naughty dogs
Y ummy food she eats
H er and me love each other
E asy to cuddle
R unning so fast I can't catch up.

Aubin Williams (7)
Hampton Pre-Prep And Prep School, Hampton

Claire My Mummy

C laire is my mummy. She

L ikes to do my brother's homework with him

A nd his reading

I really like my mummy

R eading with me

E very night!

Noah Regis (6)

Hampton Pre-Prep And Prep School, Hampton

My Daddy

D addy is very kind

A nd he eats very quick

D addy wakes up late

D addy goes to work every day

Y ummy food my daddy makes.

Max Xia (6)

Hampton Pre-Prep And Prep School, Hampton

Memoo

M y cat is really nice
E very day she gives me kisses
M y cat loves me and I love her
O pen the back door
O ff like a rocket!

Sam Wiggins (6)

Hampton Pre-Prep And Prep School, Hampton

My Cat

L ocm is my cat and she is warm and cuddly

O n Saturday she was sad

"C ome," I said, "don't be sad."

M y cat was happy and not sad.

Mahir Olcer (6)

Hampton Pre-Prep And Prep School, Hampton

Aubin

A lways a great student

U sually plays with me

B oat captain

I nteresting facts about books

N ice to know!

Alfie Seward (7)

Hampton Pre-Prep And Prep School, Hampton

Maple

M aple's lovely and friendly
A lways barking
P eas make her sick
L aps up water
E asy to cuddle!

Jack Morris (7)
Hampton Pre-Prep And Prep School, Hampton

Mango

M y cat mango is
A loved cat she
N eeds lots of cuddles
G ives cuddles and
O ften plays with me.

Theo Constanti (6)

Hampton Pre-Prep And Prep School, Hampton

Tiger

T ommy and Tiger
I love Tiger
G et him for bed
E at with me
R ough he is.

Tommy Nicholson (6)

Hampton Pre-Prep And Prep School, Hampton

The Rainforest

R unning gorillas jumping around

A nimals scurrying everywhere

I nteresting eyes, tree frogs with their blue and yellow bottoms

N aughty chimps leaping and spying on each other

F ragrant flowers making the rainforest smell nice

O range jaguars pouncing on their prey

R ivers rushing fast in the rainforest

E nemies hunting everywhere

S limy snakes slithering slowly

T reetops glisten in the rain.

Lexie-Mae Shread (7)
Robin Hood Primary School, Bestwood Park

The Rainforest

R ain dropping everywhere

A nts scurrying all over the place

I mpressive jaguars hunting for their prey

N oisy toucans being loud in the canopy

F ragrant flowers leaving a lingering smell

O rangutans swinging from branch to branch

R ivers flowing in the forest

E xcited monkeys jumping on each other

S lithering snakes sliding on the forest floor

T iny ants climbing on trees.

Shiloh Howard-Reid (6)

Robin Hood Primary School, Bestwood Park

The Rainforest

R ain falling from the sky

A nts scurrying on the forest floor

I nsects are crawling on the soil

N oisy macaws flying in the canopy

F ierce jaguars spying on their prey

O rangutans swinging from branch to branch

R iding on their mothers' backs are

E nergetic monkeys

S luggish sloths hiding in trees

T all trees have so many leaves.

Vyara Yotova (7)

Robin Hood Primary School, Bestwood Park

The Rainforest

R ainforests are humid

A mazing scaly black caimans

I nching leopards

N oisy, loud monkeys swing on trees

F urry, lazy sloths hang from tall trees

O rangutans swing from strong branch to branch

R ed-eyed tree frogs are hopping around

E normous tall trees growing

S nakes slither everywhere

T iny brown ants scatter all around.

Amy Jarzabek (6)

Robin Hood Primary School, Bestwood Park

The Rainforest

R ain falls all around
A thletic, agile jaguars
I nsects creeping around
N oisy, colourful toucans are squawking
F urry, lazy sloths hang from tall trees
O rangutans swing from branch to branch
R ed-eyed tree frogs are hopping around
E normous tall trees growing
S nakes slither everywhere
T iny brown ants scatter all around.

Lauren Clements (6)
Robin Hood Primary School, Bestwood Park

The Rainforest

R ain falls on the ground
A mazing animals hunt their prey
I nsects are busy catching food
N oisy toucans flapping their wings
F ierce jaguars roar
O rangutans jump on each other
R ivers rushing
E nergetic monkeys swing from branch to branch
S luggish sloths hang on the trees
T arantulas are sneaking around.

Sehrish Dad
Robin Hood Primary School, Bestwood Park

The Rainforest

R ain drops all around

A mazing tigers roar all around

I nsects running around

N oisy toucans squawking

F ast, fierce leopards leaping

O rangutans swing on branches

R ainforest animals having fun

E normous black caimans hunting for food

S lithering, scaly snakes are camouflaged

T iny, little leafcutter ants.

Nathaniel Oyasope (7)
Robin Hood Primary School, Bestwood Park

The Rainforest

R ain drenches the emergent layer
A mazing animals hunt for their prey
I nsects flying in the canopy
N oisy toucans squawking very loudly
F lying macaws are colourful and pretty
O range orangutans that are so excited
R acing black panthers
E nergetic cheeky monkeys
S uper fast jaguars
T all, high treetops.

Alexander Mitroi (7)

Robin Hood Primary School, Bestwood Park

The Rainforest

R ain falls all around

A mazing animals roam the forest floor

I nteresting green gecko

N oisy macaws in the canopy

F ierce jaguars watching their prey

O rangutans swinging from branch to branch

R ivers rushing

E xcited monkeys jumping on each other

S nakes slithering and sliding

T rees tumbling down.

Elijah Divall (6)

Robin Hood Primary School, Bestwood Park

The Rainforest

R ain falls fast on the ground
A mazing jaguars hunt at night
I nteresting green geckos
N oisy toucans flapping their wings
F ragrant smells from flowers
O rangutans swinging all around the place
R oaring leopards
E normous green trees wave in the wind
S tinky stingies
T ired black panthers snoozing.

Ashanti Bartley (6)

Robin Hood Primary School, Bestwood Park

The Rainforest

R ain dropping everywhere

A mazing jaguars roaring

I n the rainforest there are interesting animals

N oisy toucan squawking

F ragrant flowers leaving nice smells

O range orangutans swinging from branch to branch

R oaring leopards

S tunning macaws flapping their wings

T ree frogs showing their bottoms.

Summer-Leigh Gwynne (6)

Robin Hood Primary School, Bestwood Park

The Rainforest

R ain is falling around
A nacondas slither on the forest floor
I nsects scurry
N oisy macaws squawk
F orest flowers
O range orangutans swing from branch to branch
R ed tree frogs sleep upside down
E nergetic monkeys play with each other
S nakes slither
T ree frogs flash their bottoms.

Amir Manssour (6)

Robin Hood Primary School, Bestwood Park

The Rainforest

R ain falls all around
A nimals are waking up
I nsects crawling on the floor
N oisy, colourful macawa
F orest animals like gorillas have thick fur
O rangutans swing from tree to tree
R ough rocks
E xtremely big trees
S nakes are long and poisonous
T he long and fast cheetah is king.

Destiny Stephens (7)
Robin Hood Primary School, Bestwood Park

The Rainforest

R ain drops all around
A thletic jaguars leaping
I nteresting long snakes slithering
N oisy toucan squawking
F orests are dense and trees are close together
O rangutans swinging branch to branch
R ivers flowing
E normous trees blowing in the wind
S mall ants crawling
T rees waving.

Lacie Harvey (6)

Robin Hood Primary School, Bestwood Park

The Rainforest

R ainforest animals are running around
A nimals are hunting
I nsects crawling
N oisy, colourful toucans squawking
F ierce, strong leopards
O range, red, slimy tree frogs
R oaring tigers and slithering snakes
E normous trees
S creeching toucans and macaws flying
T rees are dense.

Rico Lowe (6)
Robin Hood Primary School, Bestwood Park

The Rainforest

R ainforests are humid

A nimals moving

I nteresting, long anacondas slithering

N ast, prickly plants

F antastic cheeky monkeys

O rangutans swing from branch to branch

R ed-eyed tree frogs are nocturnal

E normous black caimans

S limy, long snakes are coiled

T arantulas crawling.

Yishai Olaru (6)

Robin Hood Primary School, Bestwood Park

The Rainforest

R ain fall on the floor

A nimals attacking

I nsects crawling around

N oisy toucans in the canopy

F ragrant flowers smell like perfume

O rangutans are jumping from branch to branch

R oaring strong tigers

E nergetic monkeys jumping

S lithering snakes

T rees blowing in the wind.

Eli Park-Spencer (6)

Robin Hood Primary School, Bestwood Park

The Rainforest

R ain falls all around
A mazing ants are crawling
I nsects scattering
N oisy, colourful toucans
F ierce, spotty leopards sleeping
O range and red slimy frogs
R ed-eyed treed frogs are hiding
E normous, leafy trees swing over the animals
S lithering scaly snakes
T all canopy.

Hunter Simpson (6)

Robin Hood Primary School, Bestwood Park

The Rainforest

R ainforest trees are tall

A nimals hunting for their prey

I nsects crawling

N oisy, loud macaws squawking

F ierce, deadly, black caimans hiding

O rangutans swing in the trees

R ainforests are dense

E xcited animals

S lithery, slimy snakes

T he trees are long and tall.

Thomas Waterfall (6)
Robin Hood Primary School, Bestwood Park

Rainforest

R ain floods the forest

A mazing animals hunting

I n the canopy the toucans squawk

N oisy macaws flapping their wings

F ierce jaguars spying

O rangutans swinging

R ivers running slowly

E nergetic monkeys

S trong gorillas

T ree frogs bouncing on the crunchy leaves.

Thomas Bush (6)

Robin Hood Primary School, Bestwood Park

The Rainforest

R ain falls everywhere

A monkey is swinging

I n the rainforest are beautiful insects

N oisy macaws are flying

F ast leopards are pouncing

O n the trees are drops of rain

R oaring tigers

E xciting toucans

S luggish sloths

T iny tree frogs flashing their bottoms.

Lena Brzozowska (6)

Robin Hood Primary School, Bestwood Park

The Rainforest

R ain drops on the leaves

A nimals hunting for their prey

I nsects scurrying

N oisy, loud toucans squawking

F urry sloths swinging from trees

O rangutans are strong and healthy

R ainforests are dense and humid

E normous trees

S luggish, slow sloths

T all trees.

Chloe Hickling (6)

Robin Hood Primary School, Bestwood Park

The Rainforest

R ain falls on the leaves

A nteaters eat ants

I nching jaguars

N oisy, colourful toucans sqawking

F urry, lazy sloths sleeping

O n the rainforest floor the black caiman hides

R ain does not fall on the ground

E xcited monkeys

S luggish sloths

T all trees.

Alex Momoh (6)

Robin Hood Primary School, Bestwood Park

The Rainforest

R ainforest animals looking for food
A macaw is squawking loudly
I nsects looking for food
N oisy macaws
F orest leaves falling
O range leaves falling
R ain going around
E xcited animals
S nakes hunting for their prey
T all strong trees blowing.

Megan Gadsby (6)
Robin Hood Primary School, Bestwood Park

The Rainforest

R ough, bumpy rocks
A gorilla is hunting
I nsects crawling
N oisy, loud toucans squawking
F ierce and deadly black caimans
O rangutan swinging
R ough, hard rocks
E xcited animals
S low, strong, sleeping sloths
T arantulas scurrying around.

James Kpessinlo (6)
Robin Hood Primary School, Bestwood Park

The Rainforest

R ainforests are amazing
A monkey is cheeky
I nsects are scuttling
N oisy toucans flying
F ast tigers
O rangutan swinging
R ain falling around
E verything smallest in the rainforest
S mells coming from the flowers
T arantulas crawling.

La'Mour Campbell-Tucker
Robin Hood Primary School, Bestwood Park

The Rainforest

R ain falling everywhere

A nts crawling

I n the rainforest there are jaguars

N oisy toucans

F rom the leaf jumps a frog

O rangutans jumping from branch to branch

R iver rushing

E nergetic monkeys

S lithering snakes

T reetops are loud.

Milly Majstrowicz (6)
Robin Hood Primary School, Bestwood Park

The Rainforest

R ain falls around the trees
A n orangutan swings from a branch
I n the canopy toucan squawk
N aughty animals fighting
F ragrant flowers
O range orangutan
R ushing rivers
E nergetic monkeys
S lithering snakes
T rees blow in the wind.

Ellie Walters (6)

Robin Hood Primary School, Bestwood Park

The Rainforest

R ainforests are dense

A gile leopards are leaping

I nsects are crawling

N oisy, colourful macaws squawking

F ragrant flowers

O range orangutans

R ed-eyed tree frogs leaping

E normous long trees

S limy, scaly snakes

T all trees.

Mason Shelborne (6)

Robin Hood Primary School, Bestwood Park

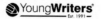
The Rainforest

R ain falls all around
A nimals screeching in the forest
I nching leopards
N oisy, colourful toucans
F ast animals
O rangutans swinging
R ough, bumpy rocks
E normous, green, leafy trees
S caly, slithering snakes
T all trees.

Esohe Irughe (7)
Robin Hood Primary School, Bestwood Park

The Rainforest

R ain is falling down

A nacondas slither around

I nsects crawling everywhere

N oisy macaws squawking

F lowers smelling beautiful

O range flowers

R ocks are hard

E nergetic leopards leaping

S trong tigers

T all trees.

Leah-Mai Haywood (6)
Robin Hood Primary School, Bestwood Park

The Rainforest

R ain falling everywhere

A nts crawling

I nsects busy working

N oisy toucans

F rogs jumping in trees

O range orangutans

R ivers rushing

E nergetic monkeys

S nakes slithering

T ree frogs show their bright bottoms.

Harley Finch (6)

Robin Hood Primary School, Bestwood Park

The Rainforest

R ainforest animals rushing about
A nacondas are slithering
I nsects creeping
N oisy, colourful toucans
F ierce leopards hunting
O rangutans swinging
R ain falling
E normous trees
S luggish sloths
T iger spying.

Eva-Lee Hallam (6)
Robin Hood Primary School, Bestwood Park

The Rainforest

R ainforest

A mazing scaly black caimans are hiding

I nching leopards

N oisy macaws squawking

F urry, lazy sloths

O rangutans in trees

R ain falling

E normous trees

S low, sluggish sloths

T arantulas crawling.

Sienna Tomlinson (7)

Robin Hood Primary School, Bestwood Park

The Rainforest

R ain drops on the ground
A nacondas slithering
I nsects scurrying
N oisy toucans
F lowers smell sweet
O range orangutans
R ivers rushing
E normous jaguars
S nakes slithering
T iny ants crawling.

Tarlia Bown (6)

Robin Hood Primary School, Bestwood Park

The Rainforest

R ainforests
A nacondas hiding
I nsects crawling
N oisy, colourful toucans
F ragrant flowers
O rangutans swing in the trees
R ain falling
E normous trees
S low sloths
T arantulas creeping.

Thomas Morley (6)
Robin Hood Primary School, Bestwood Park

The Rainforest

R ain falling

A nimals hunting

I nsects are creeping

N oisy animals

F urry orangutans

O range tree frogs

R ainforests are humid

E normous trees

S limy snails

T iny leafcutter ants.

Jenson Bentley (6) & Spencer McLean (6)

Robin Hood Primary School, Bestwood Park

The Rainforest

R aindrops falling

A nacondas slithering

I nsects crawling

N oisy toucans

F lowers smelling lovely

O range orangutan

R ed-eyed tree frog

E normous trees

S low sloths

T iny ants.

Demilee Betts (6), Cooper Carter-White (6) & Thomas Singleton (7)
Robin Hood Primary School, Bestwood Park

The Rainforest

R oar!

A mazing animals

I nsects

N aughty toucans

F ierce jaguars

O rangutans

R ivers rushing

E ating prey

S lithering snakes

T iny ants.

Tyler Singer (6)
Robin Hood Primary School, Bestwood Park

The Rainforest

R ain
A mazing animals
I nsects
N oisy
F ierce jaguar
O rangutans
R iver rushing
E ating prey
S lithering snakes
T iny ants.

Joakim Sei (7)

Robin Hood Primary School, Bestwood Park

The Rainforest

R ain
A mazing animals
I nsects
N oisy toucans
F ierce jaguar
O rangutans
R ivers rushing
E ating prey
S lithering snakes
T iny ants.

Lilly Papworth (6), Andrea, Nevaeh & Maia Goslawski (6)
Robin Hood Primary School, Bestwood Park

My Pet

G uinea pigs are cute
U nderground is where guinea pigs live
I n their home, we clean them out on Wednesdays
N ice guinea pigs
E ven guinea pigs need extra food
A nd hay and straw

P ets like seeing you
I nside their homes they eat vegetables
G reat guinea pigs.

Edward Murphy (6)
St Andrew's CE Primary School, Shifnal

Charlie

C harlie is a fox

H e does walk on the lead

A nd eats food

R eally soft

L ikes bones

I s good every day

E ven at night

F luffy friend

O nly talks to me

X -rays not needed.

Rowan Oates (5)

St Andrew's CE Primary School, Shifnal

My Family

M um and Dad love me so much
Y ou like them

F amily is the best
A lways looking after me
M um, we look after each other
I can sleep in her bed
L oves me
Y es I love them too.

Luka Brazier (5)
St Andrew's CE Primary School, Shifnal

Big Bunny

B ig and soft

I love him

G orgeous he is, I'm telling the truth

B rave and loving

U nbelievably handsome

N ever question him

N icest person I've met

Y ou're the best!

Bethany Deavall (6)

St Andrew's CE Primary School, Shifnal

All The Teachers!

T he teachers are...
E xciting and have fun ideas
A nd have tried very hard
C areful and
H elp us when we're hurt
E ven sometimes letting us
R est but not all the time
S till awesome!

Jasper Edwards (6)
St Andrew's CE Primary School, Shifnal

Sniffet

S niff, sniff, dogs sniff

N aughty dogs eat socks

I mpatient for dog food

F luffy, fluffy dogs

F ood, dog food is what they eat

E xcited when people come in

T idy, tidy dog room.

Emiko Leese (6)
St Andrew's CE Primary School, Shifnal

Pedro

P ug, playful, he is a black one

E ats dog food and is quite smelly

D ogs are amazing. He is a boy and likes to play ball

R uffs at dogs, cars, anything. He is

O paque, you can't see through him.

Phoebe Clarke (7)
St Andrew's CE Primary School, Shifnal

Granny

G ranny sometimes gives me ice cream

R unning with my granny

A nd Granny sometimes goes to her friend's house

N ext I have dinner at my granny's

N ormally she bakes with me

Y ummy cakes.

Ben Whale (5)
St Andrew's CE Primary School, Shifnal

Riminie

R iminie is a very good friend
I nteresting to talk with
M akes me feel happy
I ncredible to play with
N ice at all times
I n my garden at all times
E xcellent friend.

Hattie Brettle (6)
St Andrew's CE Primary School, Shifnal

Popsicle

P oppy is my cat
O n her bed she curls up
P aws with claws
S harp too
I love her so much
C lever cat
L ikes her food a lot
E very morning she eats.

Charlie Callis (5)
St Andrew's CE Primary School, Shifnal

Edward

E ating good every day

D oing good always

W orking hard every day

A lways brilliant each day

R ocking every day on his drum

D rumming each day, not missing a day.

Will Elsmore-Roberts (5)

St Andrew's CE Primary School, Shifnal

My Fish Called Bubble

B ubble is fun to play with
U nder the seaweed he lies down
B eautiful and kind
B ubble loves me and he is cute
L ies down a lot
E very day he's pretty too.

Hettie Middleton (6)
St Andrew's CE Primary School, Shifnal

My Dogs

M y dogs like me
Y ou can feed them

D ogs always go bark!
O h dogs, they get muddy
G oing with my dogs will make me happy
S o dogs are very good.

Oliver Snowdon-Cox (6)

St Andrew's CE Primary School, Shifnal

Connie

C rafty and very good at painting
O bsessed with strawberries
N ice and kind
N ever mean to me
I ncredibly cool clothes
E xcellent friend.

Evie Stanford (6)

St Andrew's CE Primary School, Shifnal

Daddy

D addy takes me up to bed
A nd puts the washing out
D addy loves me and my brother
D addy helps cook the dinner
Y es he is the best daddy.

Mia Gailey (6)
St Andrew's CE Primary School, Shifnal

Blake

B est friend Blake
L ikes to play football with me
A nd he's super kind, helpful and lovely
K ind friend forever
E njoy playing together.

James Simpson (7)
St Andrew's CE Primary School, Shifnal

Doctors

D octors are kind

O h so awesome

C an help so much

T o help you stay safe

O ur lives will be saved

R eally help people.

Alfie Danby (6)

St Andrew's CE Primary School, Shifnal

Heidi

H eidi is our cat

E very day she eats our food

I n the front room

D own at the bottom of the stairs

I s where the litter tray is!

Louise Pearson (6)

St Andrew's CE Primary School, Shifnal

Lamby

L amby helps me when I'm upset
A mazing friend
M e and him are best friends
B ecause I love him
Y ou are my best friend, Lamby.

Bea Edwards Sherwood (6)

St Andrew's CE Primary School, Shifnal

My Dog

M y dog is Bailey
Y ou are the best dog I have

D igging lots of times
O ver the park you run away
G rowling outside.

Alfie Ashley (6)
St Andrew's CE Primary School, Shifnal

My Fish Orange

O ld, 70

R ude sometimes

A ngry all the time

N aughty because he hides from me

G rumpy

E ats food all the time.

Eden Hateley (6)
St Andrew's CE Primary School, Shifnal

Jessy

J essy is kind
E verything she does I appreciate
S he helps me
S he is a gamer, a bit like me
Y es, she is quite like me.

Molly-May Chapman (7)

St Andrew's CE Primary School, Shifnal

Chloe

C hloe lets me come for a sleepover
H igh chairs
L ottie has a box that disappears
O h, fairies in her room
E verywhere!

Isabella Turner (5)
St Andrew's CE Primary School, Shifnal

My Dogs

M y dogs are lovely
Y oghurt they eat

D ogs, they are cute
O h so cute
G rowling
S itting for treats.

Ivy Hawkes (6)

St Andrew's CE Primary School, Shifnal

James

J ames is my brother
A lways drawing animals
M akes me feel good
E ight is his next birthday
S illy faces he pulls.

Liam Simpson (5)

St Andrew's CE Primary School, Shifnal

Mummy

M akes dinner

U p to bed

M y mummy takes me out

M ummy picks me up from school

Y ummy cakes that Mummy makes.

Jack Parry (6)

St Andrew's CE Primary School, Shifnal

Phoebe

P retty and lovely

H elpful and kind

O n the park we play

E xciting girl

B eautiful

E xcellent girl.

Oliver Poole (6)

St Andrew's CE Primary School, Shifnal

Connor

C onnor is my brother

O n my side

N early all the time

N ever snores

O n the weekend

R uns with me.

Joanna Doyle (5)

St Andrew's CE Primary School, Shifnal

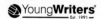

Lewis

L ewis is my cousin

E xcited when Chelsea play

W ears cool clothes

I ncredible cousin

S upports Chelsea.

Leo Stevens (6)

St Andrew's CE Primary School, Shifnal

Tommy

T ommy plays with me
O range he loves like me
M ake Lego together
M ake pretend food
Y ummy chocolate cake!

Alfie Tappenden (5)
St Andrew's CE Primary School, Shifnal

Daddy

D addy makes me laugh

A nd sometimes

D addy is funny

D on't eat too many biscuits

Y esterday he read to me.

William Drew (5)

St Andrew's CE Primary School, Shifnal

Evie

E vie my sister

V ery kind and helpful

I mpatient when we have to queue to go on a plane

E very day she plays with me.

Alfie Stanford (6)

St Andrew's CE Primary School, Shifnal

My Cat

M y cat is fluffy
Y ou cheer up my day

C ute and cuddly
A nd purring away
T ail twitching to play.

Louie Harris (7)
St Andrew's CE Primary School, Shifnal

Mummy

M y mummy gives me ice cream
U p to bed
M ummy lets me see the moon
M ummy loves me
Y ou are always good.

Penny Robinson (5)

St Andrew's CE Primary School, Shifnal

George

G eorge is nice to me
E very day
O ranges he eats
R ushes around
G iggles a lot
E very day.

William Fellows (5)
St Andrew's CE Primary School, Shifnal

Mummy

M ummy hugs me

U pstairs in her bed

M ummy reads me stories

M akes me cakes

Y ou would like them too.

Sia Archontis-Soultana (5)

St Andrew's CE Primary School, Shifnal

Mummy

M ummy bakes with me

U p to bed with Mummy

M ummy loves me

M ummy plays with me

Y ummy cakes.

Freya Gallimore (5)

St Andrew's CE Primary School, Shifnal

Daddy

D addy gives me cuddles
A nd plays games
D addy plays football
D addy helps me
Y ou are the best!

Alfie Evans (6)
St Andrew's CE Primary School, Shifnal

Mummy

M ummy loves me

U nderstands me

M ummy sometimes gets mad

M axine is her name

Y ou are beautiful.

Charlie Jones (5)

St Andrew's CE Primary School, Shifnal

Alexa

A lexa is lovely

L oves me too

E specially when I'm with her

X -rays not yet

A lways she is good.

Kasper Giddings (5)

St Andrew's CE Primary School, Shifnal

Mummy

M ummy takes me

U p to bed

M ummy takes me to the park

M ummy brings me to school

Y ou love me.

Riley Setter (6)
St Andrew's CE Primary School, Shifnal

Toto

T oto sometimes cries at night
O n my bed he will sleep
T oys sometimes broken
O n his walks he goes fast.

Faith Hepburn (5)
St Andrew's CE Primary School, Shifnal

Daddy

D addy cuddles me
A nd plays with me
D addy cooks food
D addy puts me to bed
Y es Daddy!

Yonni Saffhill (5)

St Andrew's CE Primary School, Shifnal

Lola

L oving friend and kind
O n the playground we play
L ovely and friendly
A nd my friend is so beautiful.

Eve Kolaric (6)
St Andrew's CE Primary School, Shifnal

Jack

J ack is very funny
A nd he likes to play and run
C ute Jack, he is lovely
K ind Jack, he likes Mummy.

Luke Hayward (6)

St Andrew's CE Primary School, Shifnal

Freya

F reya helps me

R eads with me

E veryone helps Daisy

Y ou are the best

A nd a good friend.

Daisy Davis (5)

St Andrew's CE Primary School, Shifnal

Mummy

M agnificent Mummy
U nbelievably kind
M agic
M oody sometimes
Y ummy dinners she cooks.

Edward Jackson (6)
St Andrew's CE Primary School, Shifnal

My Brother

J acob is my brother

A nd he is the best brother

C ute

O range hair

B est brother ever!

Olivia Hartshorn-Jones (5)
St Andrew's CE Primary School, Shifnal

Evie

E vie is so kind
V ery funny and nice
I think that
E vie is friendly.

Connie Morgans Sharples (6)

St Andrew's CE Primary School, Shifnal

Ray

R ay loves to cuddle people
A nd jumps up at new people
Y ou would love him.

Drew Hodgkisson (5)
St Andrew's CE Primary School, Shifnal

Roman

R olling
O n the floor
M oves
A round
N oisy.

Cooper Arnold (5)

St Andrew's CE Primary School, Shifnal

God

G od made everywhere

O utside God made everything

D ogs from God.

Finley Hanwell

St Andrew's CE Primary School, Shifnal

Abby

A bby sometimes is good

B ossy

B ig sister

Y uck!

Jacob Morris (6)

St Andrew's CE Primary School, Shifnal

Eve

E ve is helpful

V ery funny

E xciting and kind and friendly.

Lola Underwood (6)

St Andrew's CE Primary School, Shifnal

Ivy

I like Ivy
V ery friendly
Y ellow hair.

Lauren Owen (6)

St Andrew's CE Primary School, Shifnal

Seb

S leep
E at
B ath.

Olivia Timon (5)

St Andrew's CE Primary School, Shifnal

Family

F amilies are good for us because families love us

A nimals have families too

M y family is kind to me

I s there other families who are kind to their children?

L ove my family so much

Y es, I love my family to the moon and back.

Erin Stead (6)

Woodlands Academy Of Learning, Willenhall

Everest Is My Sister

E   verest is a dog

V   ets take care of her

E   v I call her sometimes

R   est, she does rest

E   verest is my sister

S   he is my favourite sister

T   he rule to me is to protect her.

Tyler Godwin (7)

Woodlands Academy Of Learning, Willenhall

The Family Poem

F amily always makes me smile
A family is nice to have
M y family are always kind
I never choose bad things for my family
L ife is nice with family
Y ou're the best!

Noah Davies-Johnson (6)

Woodlands Academy Of Learning, Willenhall

Friends

F un and smiles
R eally fun
I like to play with them
E ver, friends forever
N ever ever break up
D o we love each other?
S o do we like gymnastics?

Chante Richards (6)

Woodlands Academy Of Learning, Willenhall

Simber

S imber is the cutest bunny

I know

M y mum always says, "No Simber!"

B lue-eyed Simber

E xcellent at jumping

R uns outside.

Jorgie Moore-Butler (6)

Woodlands Academy Of Learning, Willenhall

Family

F un and nice

A lways making me smile

M om, Dad, Nan and Grandad

I 'll always love them

L oving is caring

Y ummy food they make.

Zack Dempsey (6)

Woodlands Academy Of Learning, Willenhall

Friend

F riends are like family

R eally helpful

I can be with my friend

E xcited friends

N ever alone

D ress up with your friends.

Isabelle Smith (6)

Woodlands Academy Of Learning, Willenhall

Eddie And Me

E xciting, fun, kind and friendly

D ances all the time

D reaming every night

I ndependent every day at school

E ddie is the best!

Poppy Bird (7)

Woodlands Academy Of Learning, Willenhall

Friend Poem

C aterpillars are her favourite
H eart to heart
A for awesome
N ever leave her side
T reats together
E at together.

Ivy Young (6)

Woodlands Academy Of Learning, Willenhall

Poppy

P oppy flowers are cute
O laf is made out of snow
P oppy B is made my friend
P oppy J is my friend
Y ou are eating pizza.

Tallulah Webster (7)

Woodlands Academy Of Learning, Willenhall

The Caring Sister

L ove you every day

A dventure and wonder

U s together

R usty and Ruby we watch together

A dvice and care you give me.

Rosie Morris (7)

Woodlands Academy Of Learning, Willenhall

Minnie

M y teddy

I s the best at

N ight she keeps me warm

N ever ever lose her

I love you

E ach night I hug you.

Poppy Jackson (6)

Woodlands Academy Of Learning, Willenhall

Friend

F riends play

R ead books

I nside we relax

E at together

N ever alone

D ance to songs together.

Amelia Parke (6)

Woodlands Academy Of Learning, Willenhall

Books

B ooks are amazing

O h look, best book

O n we go book

K eep the book

S o now I'm finished at the library.

Mia Phillips (6)

Woodlands Academy Of Learning, Willenhall

Books

B asketball is the best
O ctober is good
O nce upon a time
K itKats are tasty
S nakes are nice.

Harry Edwards (6)
Woodlands Academy Of Learning, Willenhall

Sun

S un is hot and summer is really hot
U mbrella gives you shade when it is sunny
N o more sunburn on the beach.

Isaac Julie (6)
Woodlands Academy Of Learning, Willenhall

The Best Cousin

L ola is my best cousin
O n her phone all day
L ola is beautiful
A nd she laughs with me all day.

Emily Davies (7)
Woodlands Academy Of Learning, Willenhall

Books

B ooks are awesome

O h look at that book

O n we go to the adventure

K eep practising reading.

Lydia Bate (6)

Woodlands Academy Of Learning, Willenhall

Amy

A mber is my best friend ever

M y sister's name is Amy

Y ou might see her in Gran Canaria.

Oliver Clare (7)

Woodlands Academy Of Learning, Willenhall

My Pet Oreo

O reo is my pet
R eal cutie every day
E very day she is the best
O reo is cute.

Eloise Wainwright (6)
Woodlands Academy Of Learning, Willenhall

Love

L ove you

O ne person is loved

V ery friendly

E verything is awesome.

Amber Handley (7)

Woodlands Academy Of Learning, Willenhall

Bugs

B ugs are small
U nder the grass
G ot to watch out for them
S ting.

Thomas-Jay Kennedy (6)

Woodlands Academy Of Learning, Willenhall

Birds

B ig birds
I n the sky
R esting in the garden
D ig in the grass.

Ekam Dhaliwal (6)

Woodlands Academy Of Learning, Willenhall

Lion

L ions roar
I n the grass
O range and yellow
N ot good.

Riley Hayes (7)

Woodlands Academy Of Learning, Willenhall

Sun

S himmering sun in the blue sky
U mbrella gives us shade
N o sand.

Ava Worgan (6)
Woodlands Academy Of Learning, Willenhall

Dog

D ogs are cute
O bjects are what she likes
G reat dog.

Jessica Hammond (6)
Woodlands Academy Of Learning, Willenhall

Mum

M y mum cleans
U ses the hoover
M um is the best.

Theo Harris (6)
Woodlands Academy Of Learning, Willenhall

Bob

B eautiful

O bjects, he likes them

B lack.

Paige Cooper (6)

Woodlands Academy Of Learning, Willenhall

Young Writers Information

We hope you have enjoyed reading this book – and that you will continue to in the coming years.

If you're a young writer who enjoys reading and creative writing, or the parent of an enthusiastic poet or story writer, do visit our website **www.youngwriters.co.uk**. Here you will find free competitions, workshops and games, as well as recommended reads, a poetry glossary and our blog. There's lots to keep budding writers motivated to write!

If you would like to order further copies of this book, or any of our other titles, then please give us a call or order via your online account.

Young Writers
Remus House
Coltsfoot Drive
Peterborough
PE2 9BF
(01733) 890066
info@youngwriters.co.uk

Join in the conversation!
Tips, news, giveaways and much more!

 YoungWritersUK    @YoungWritersCW